SCISSOR SKILLS

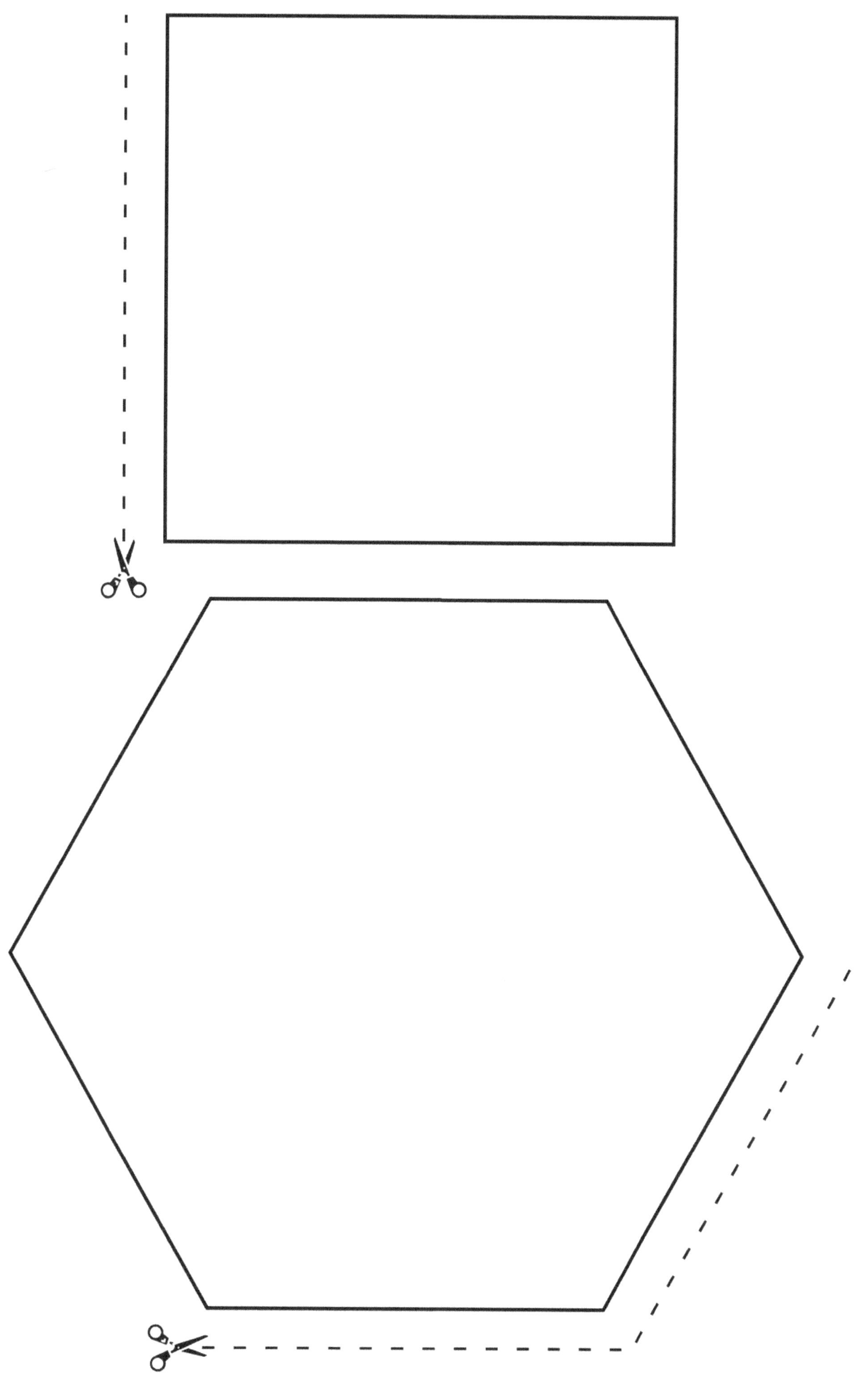

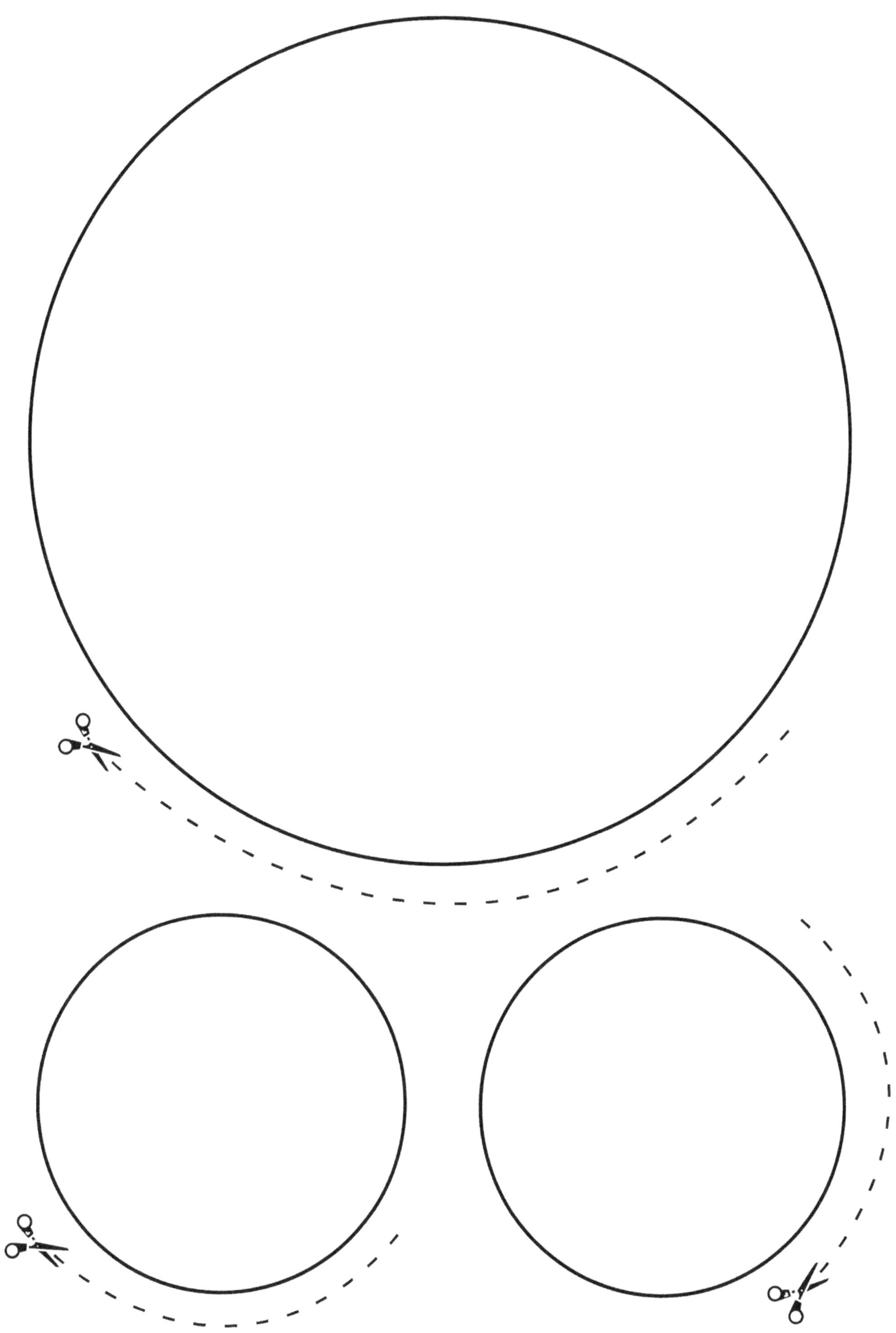

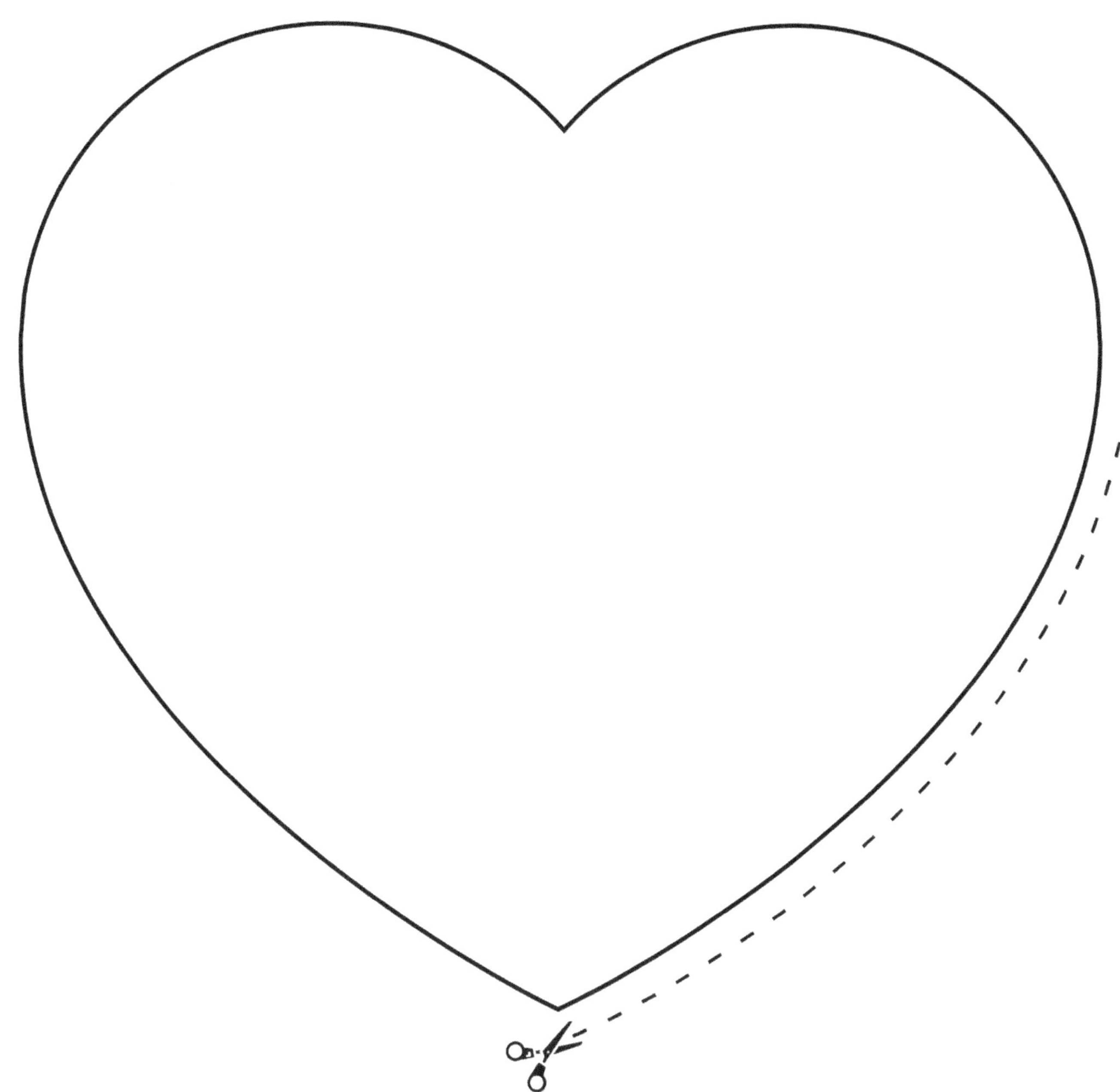

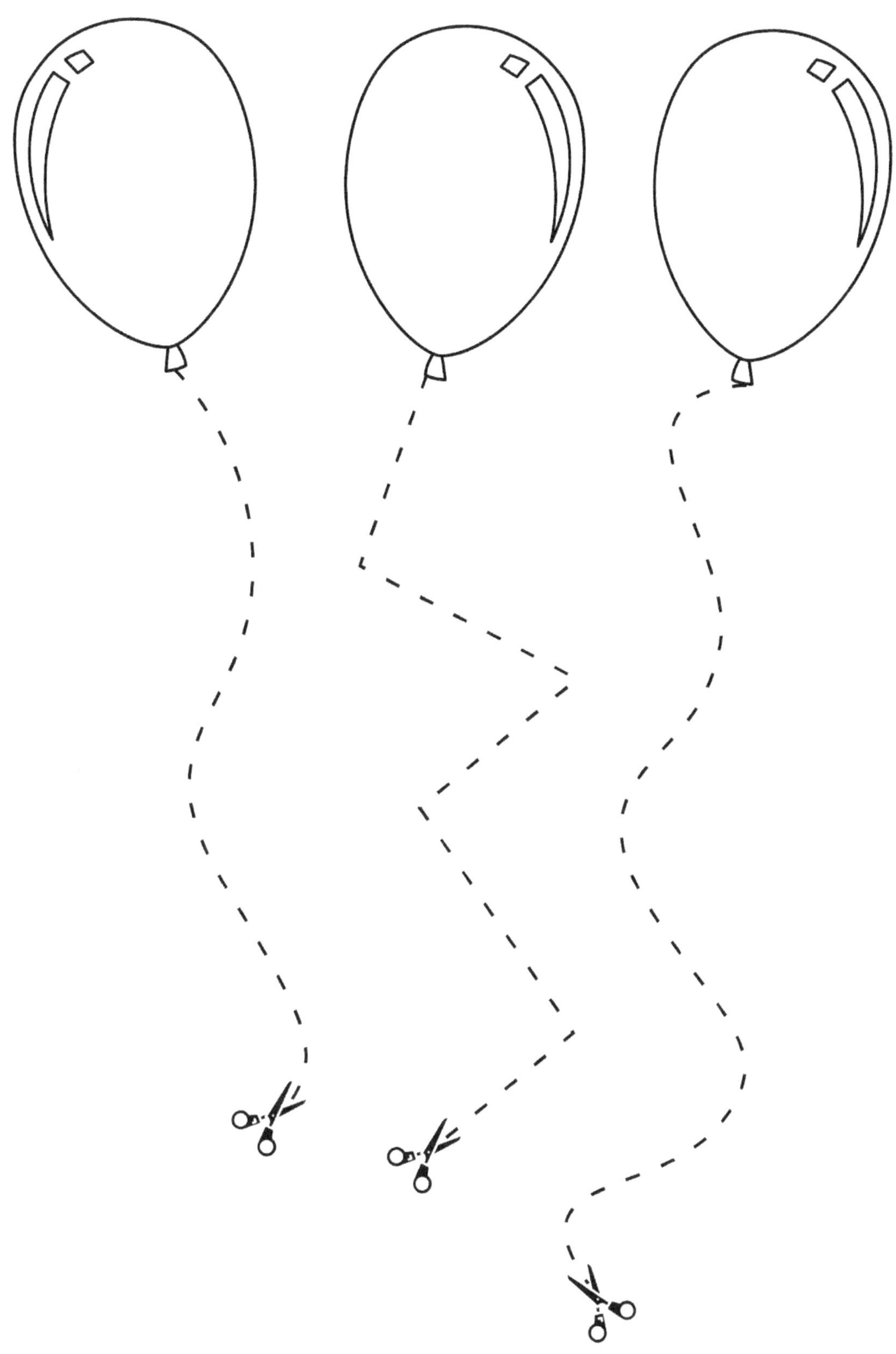

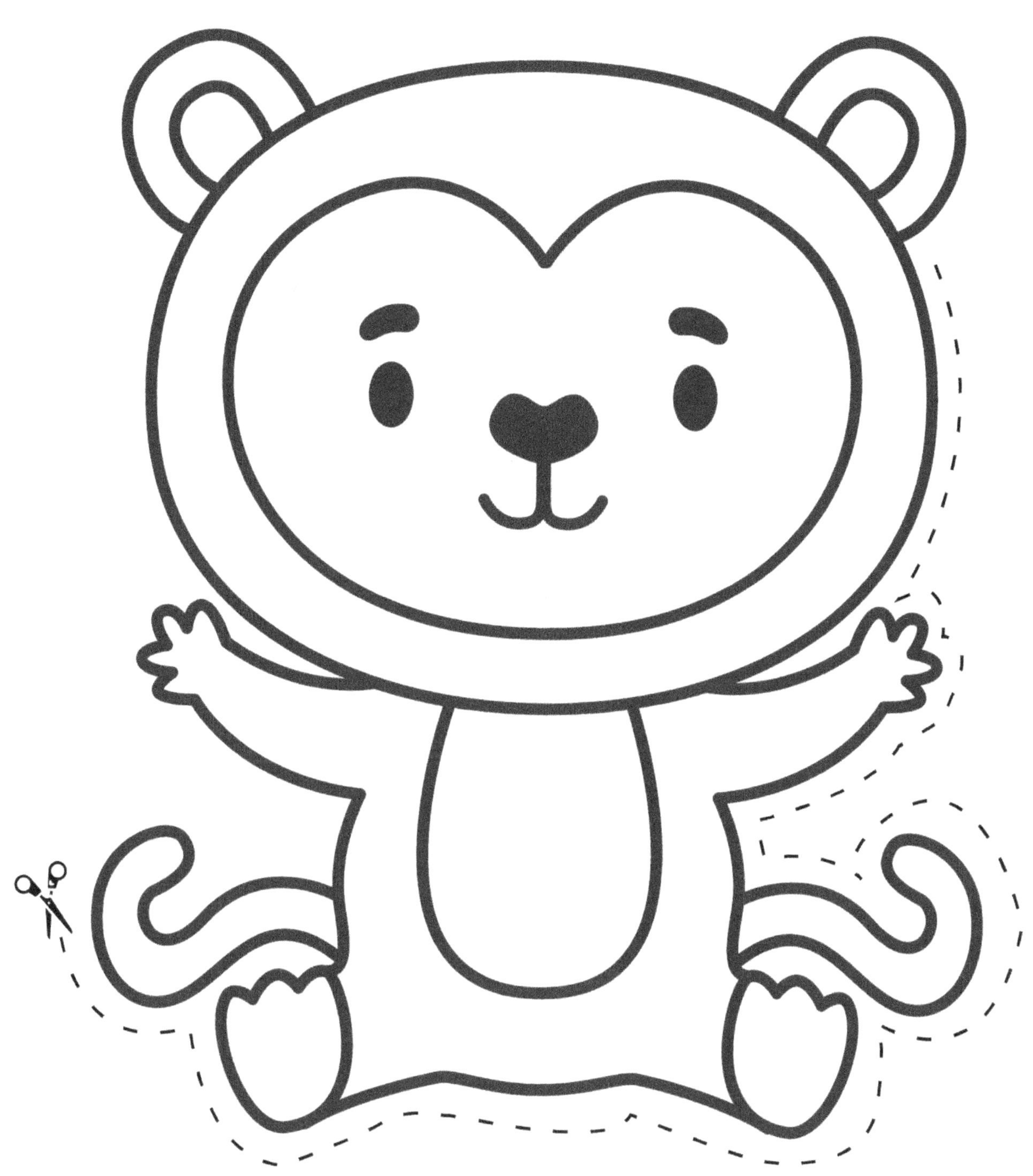

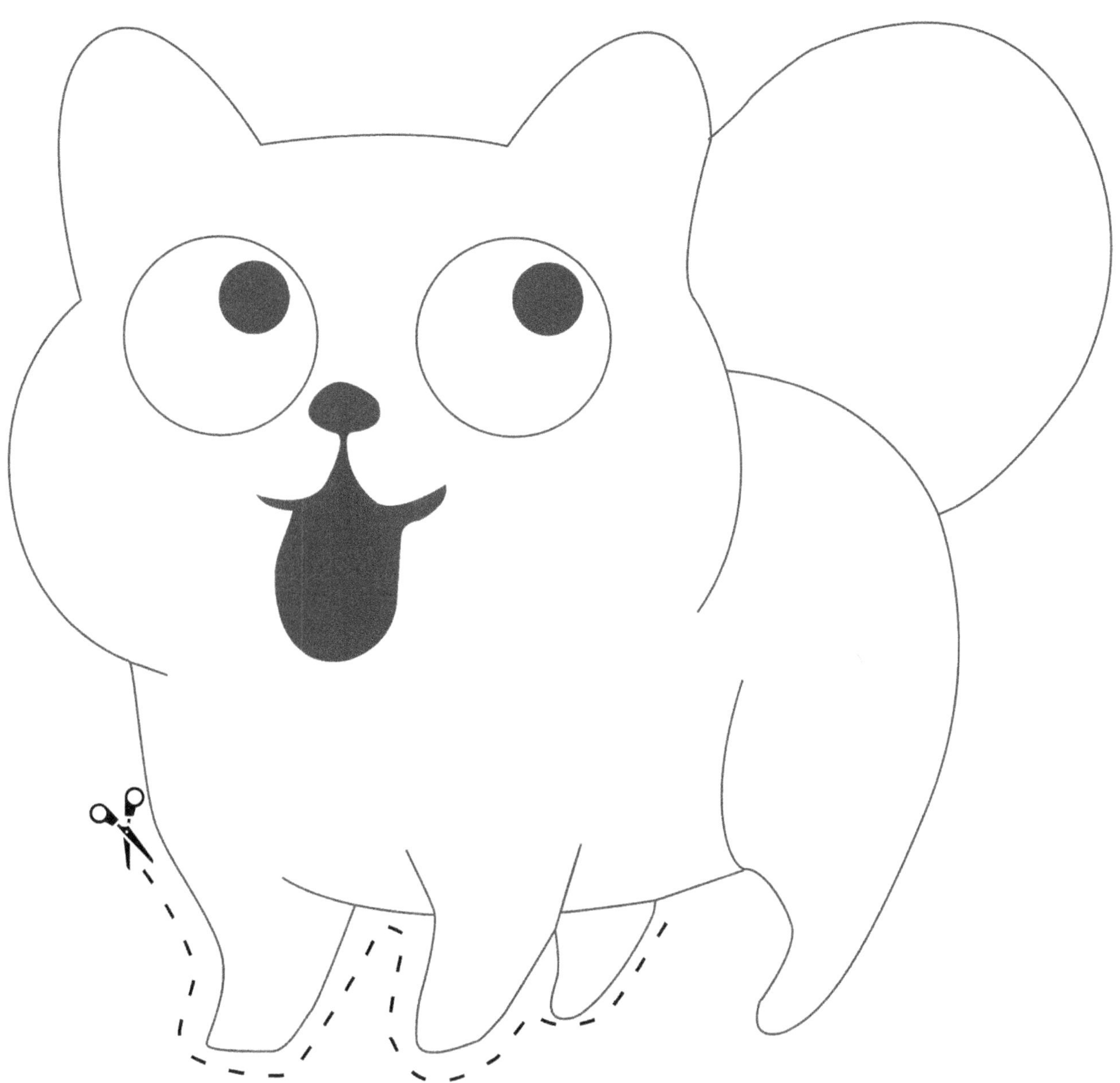

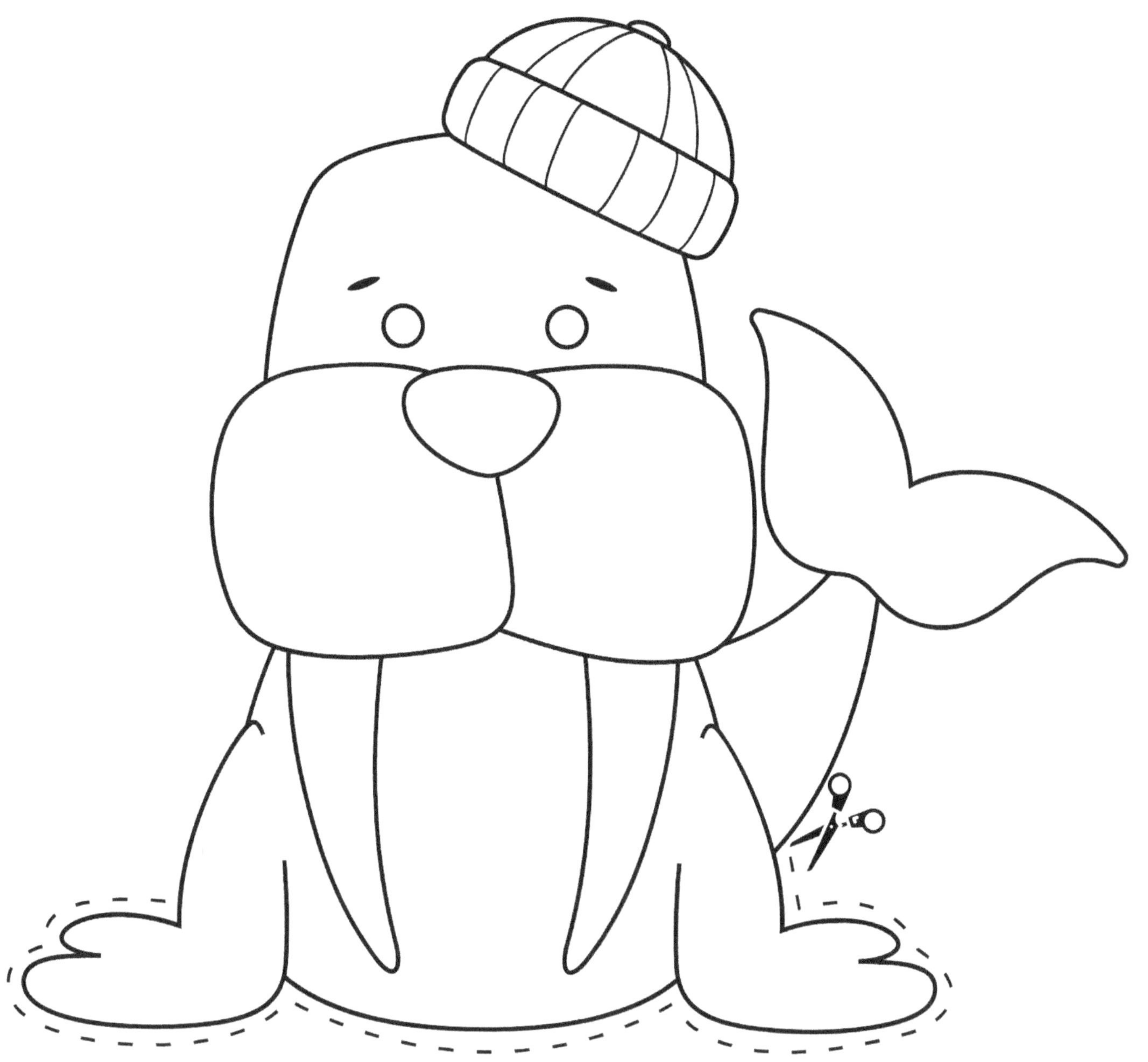

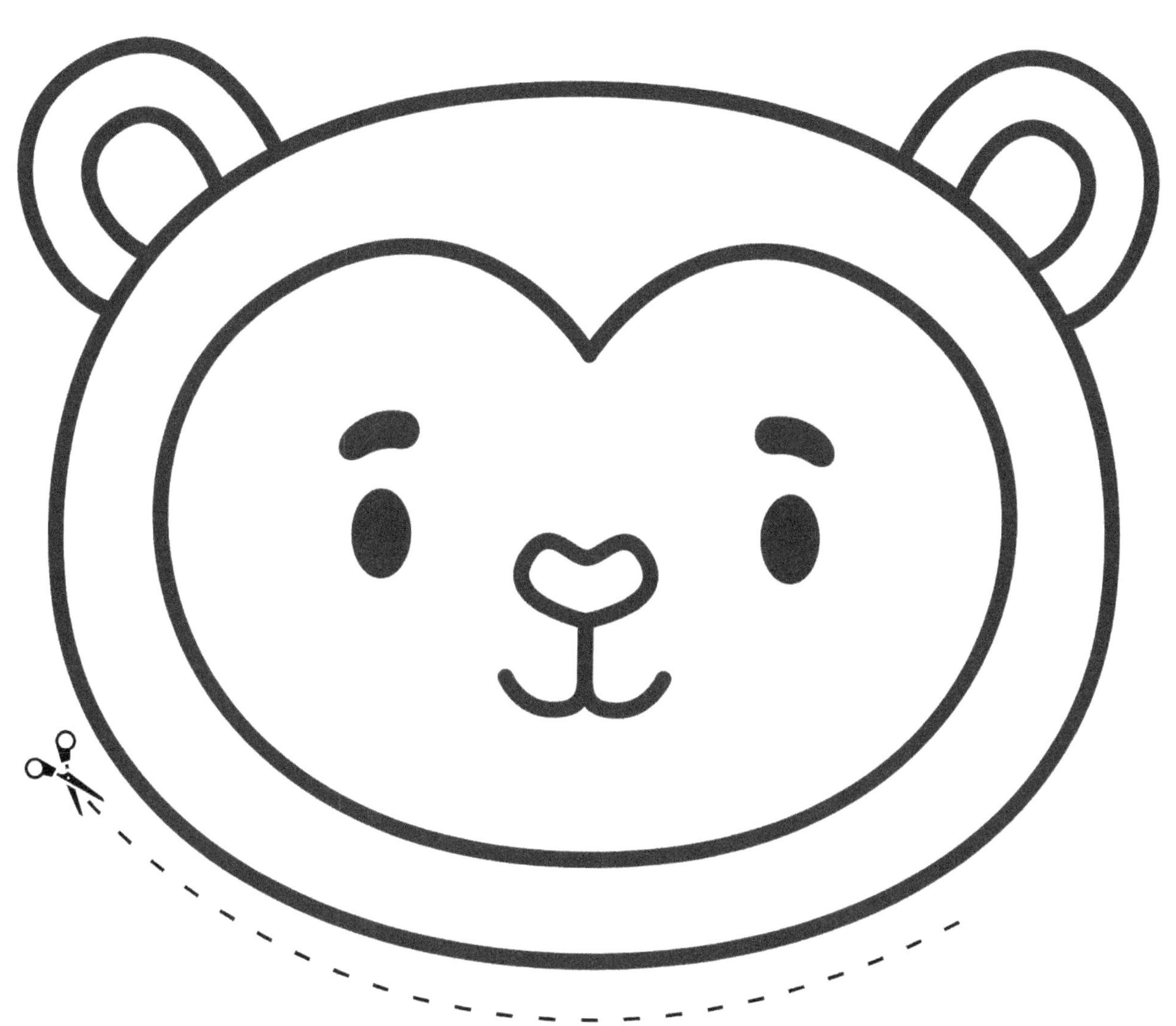

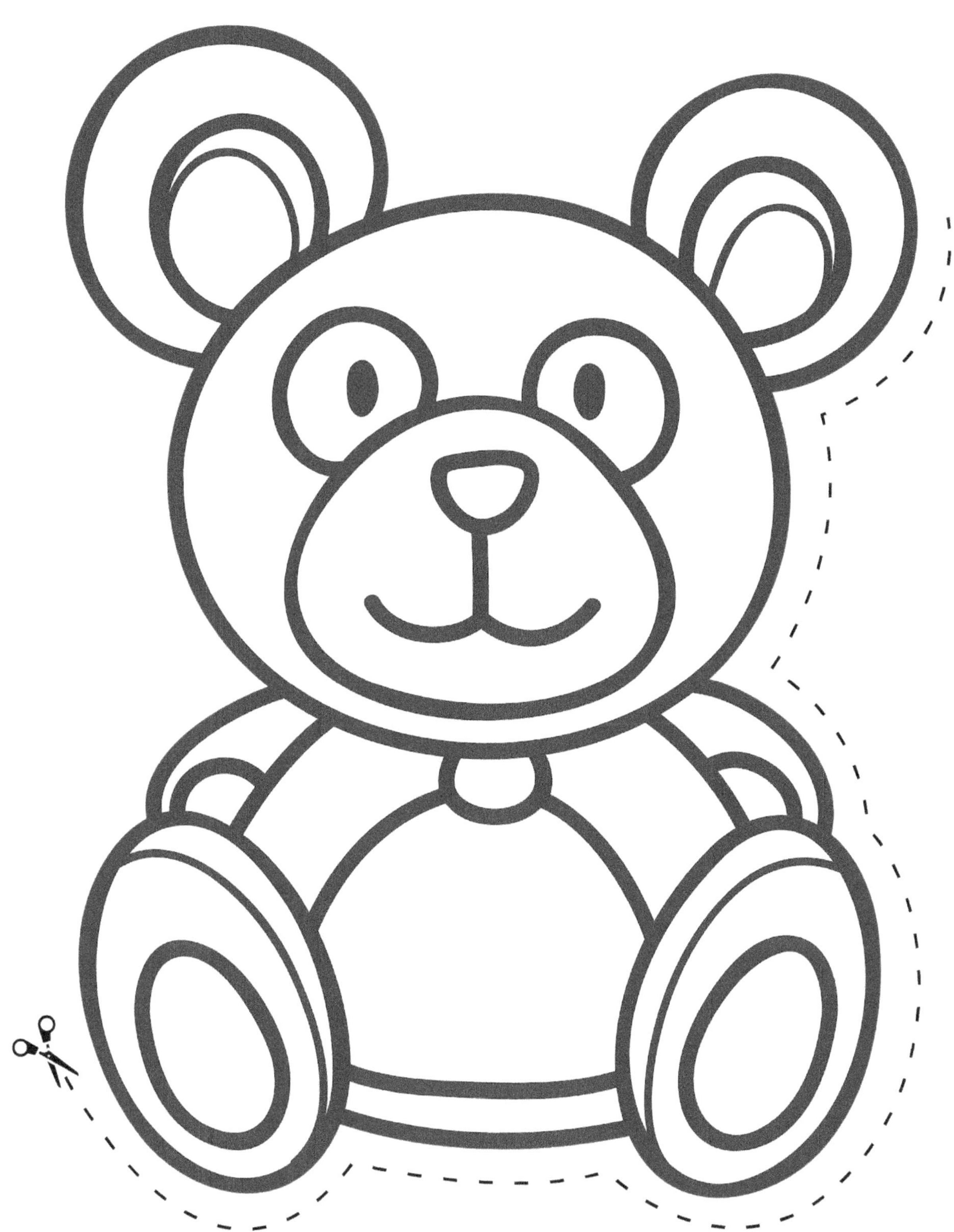

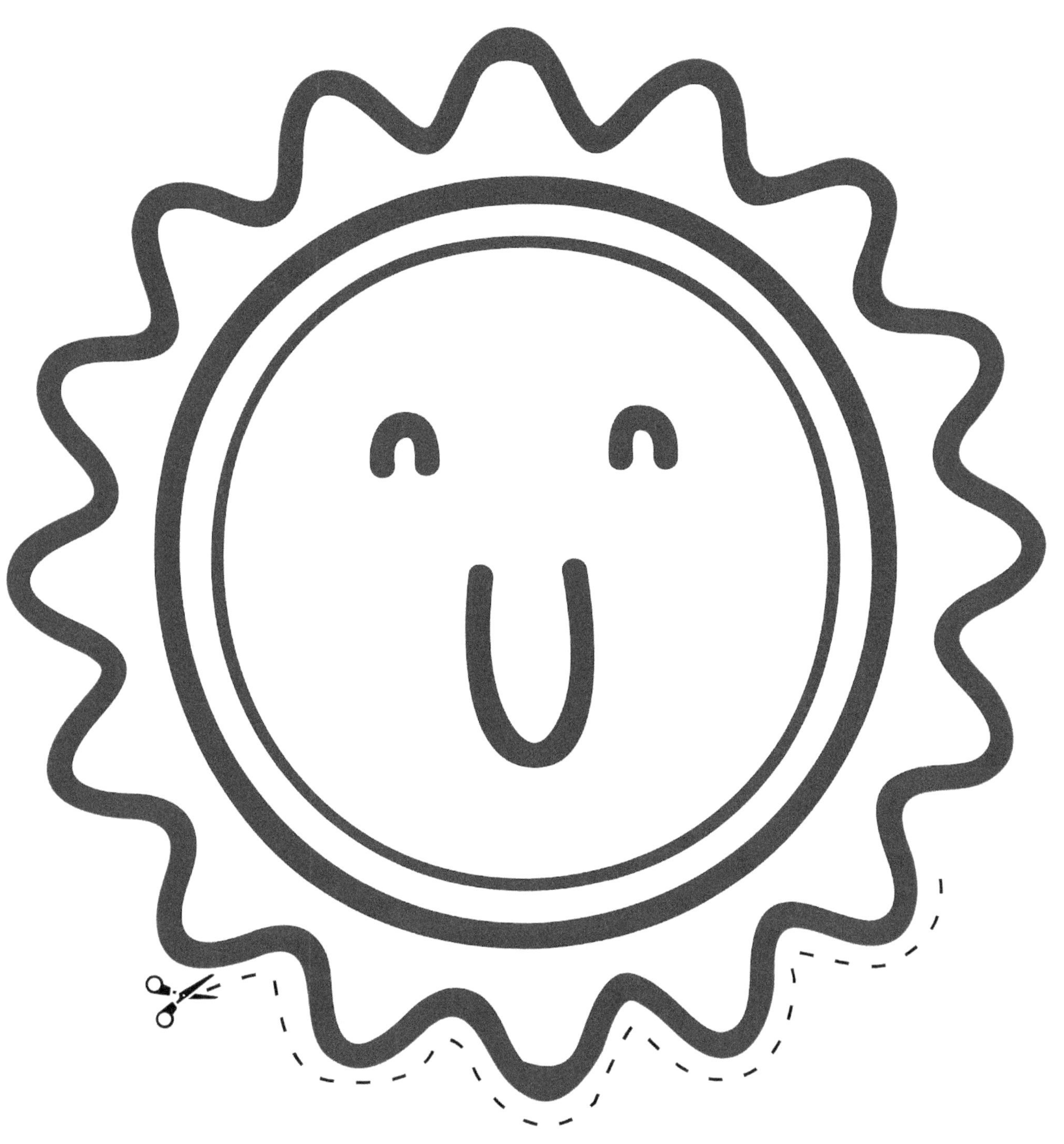

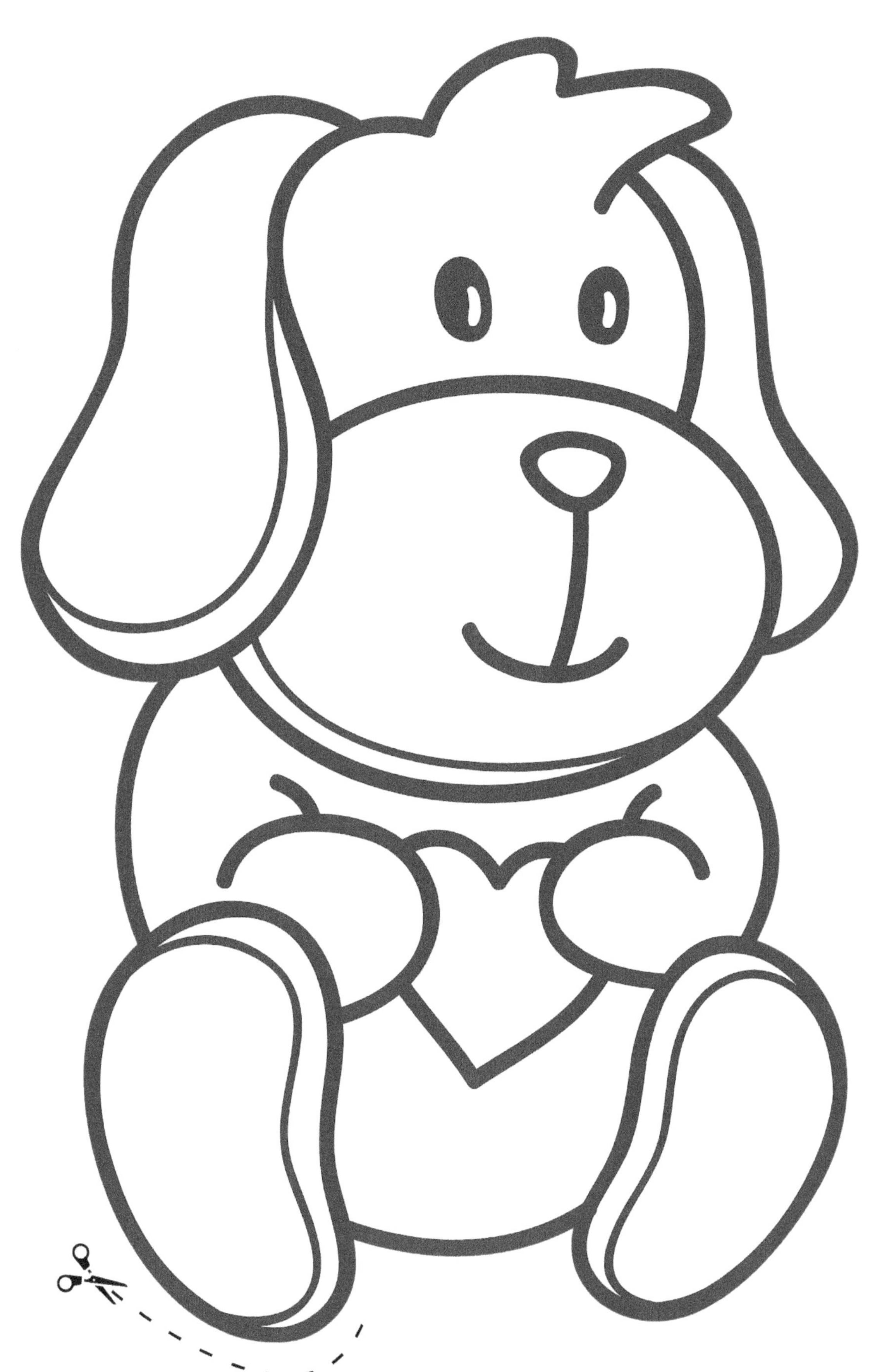

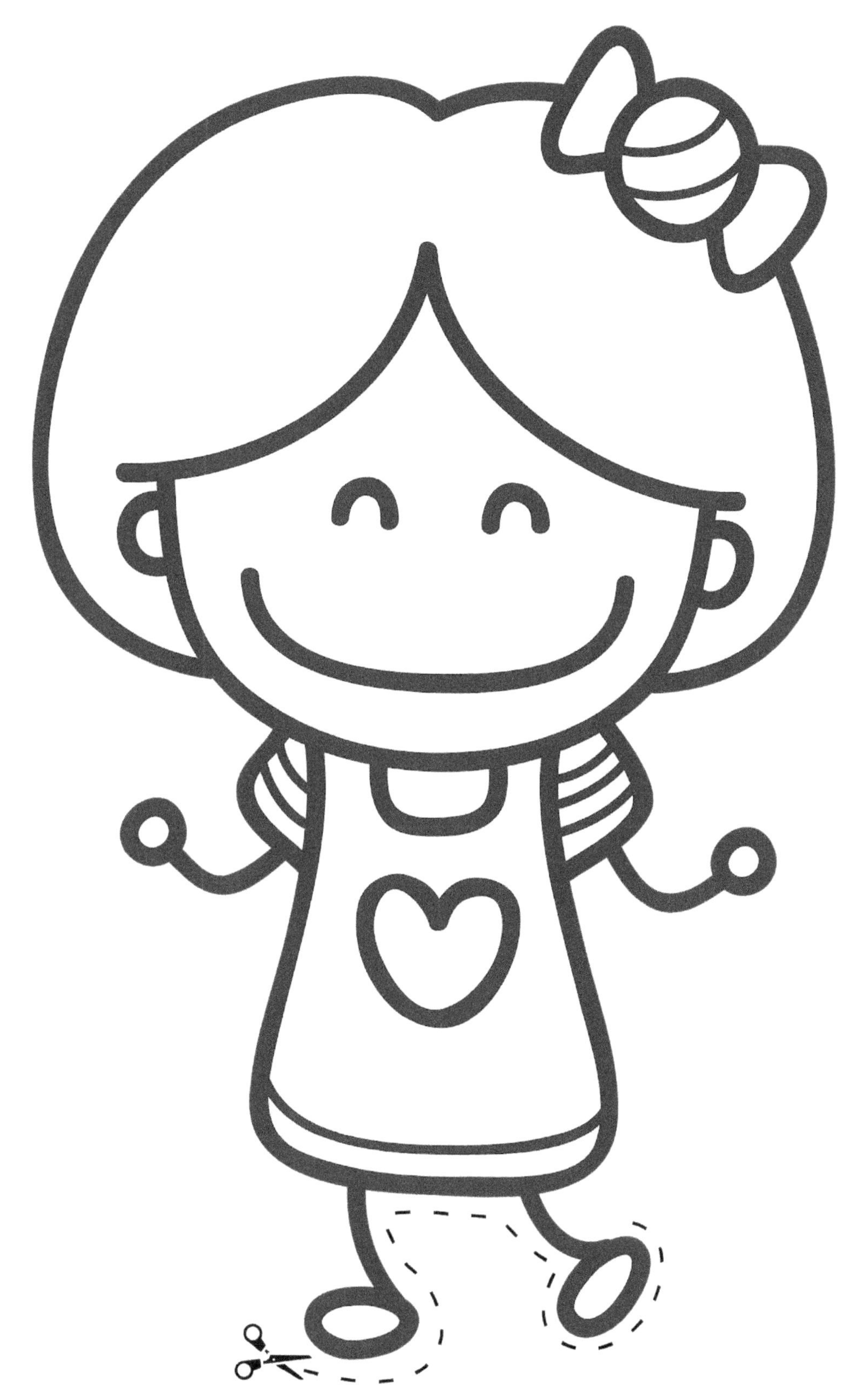

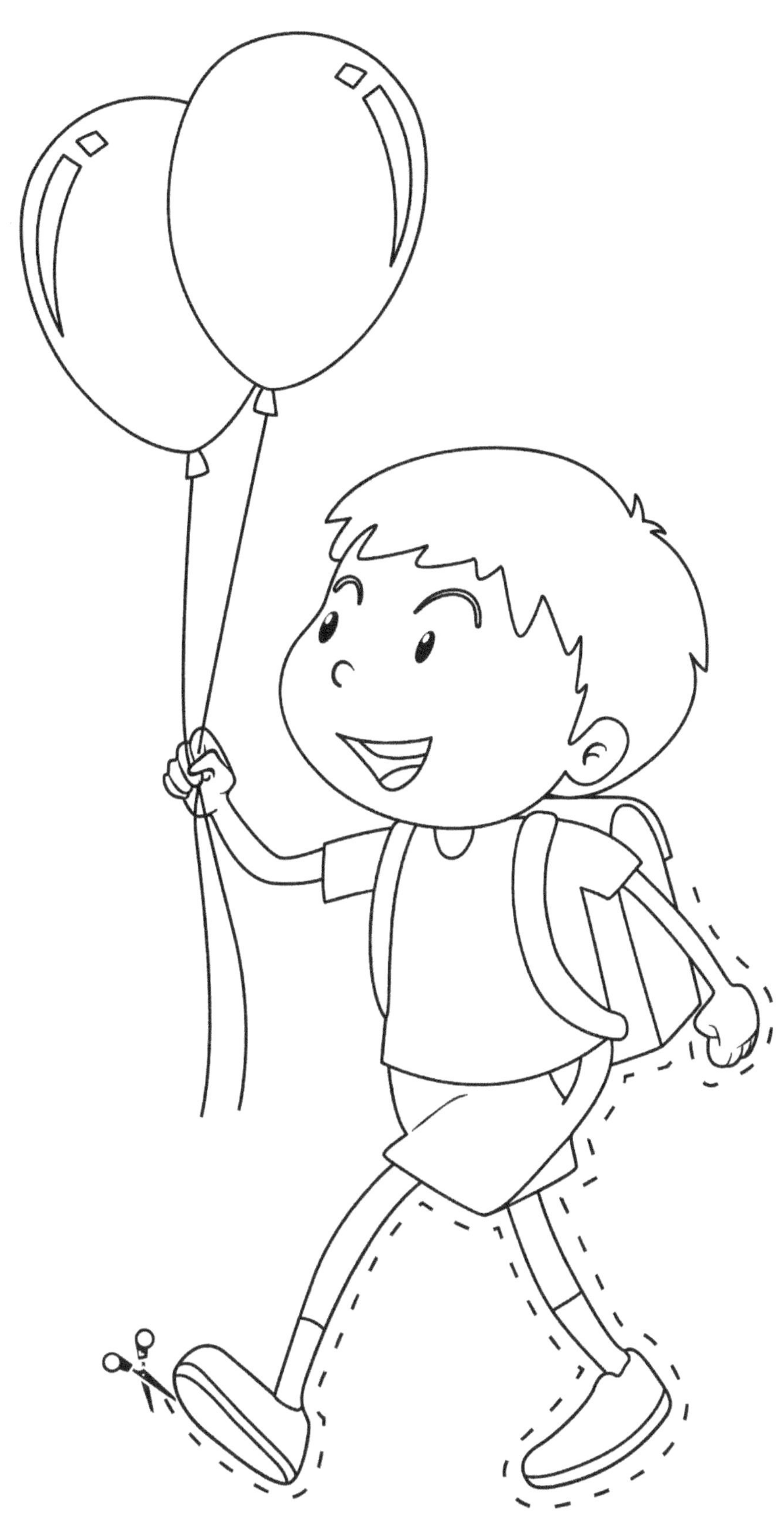

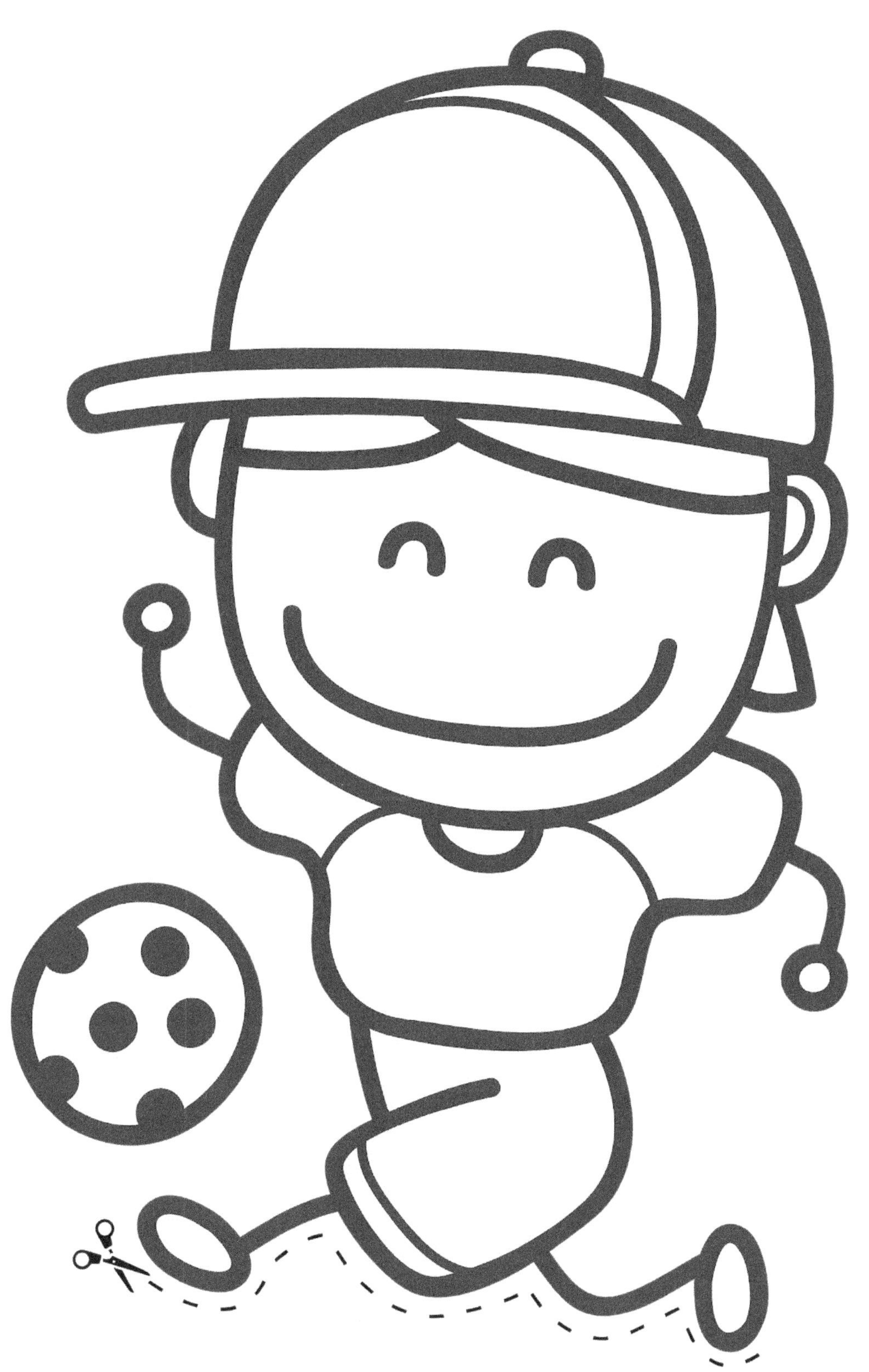

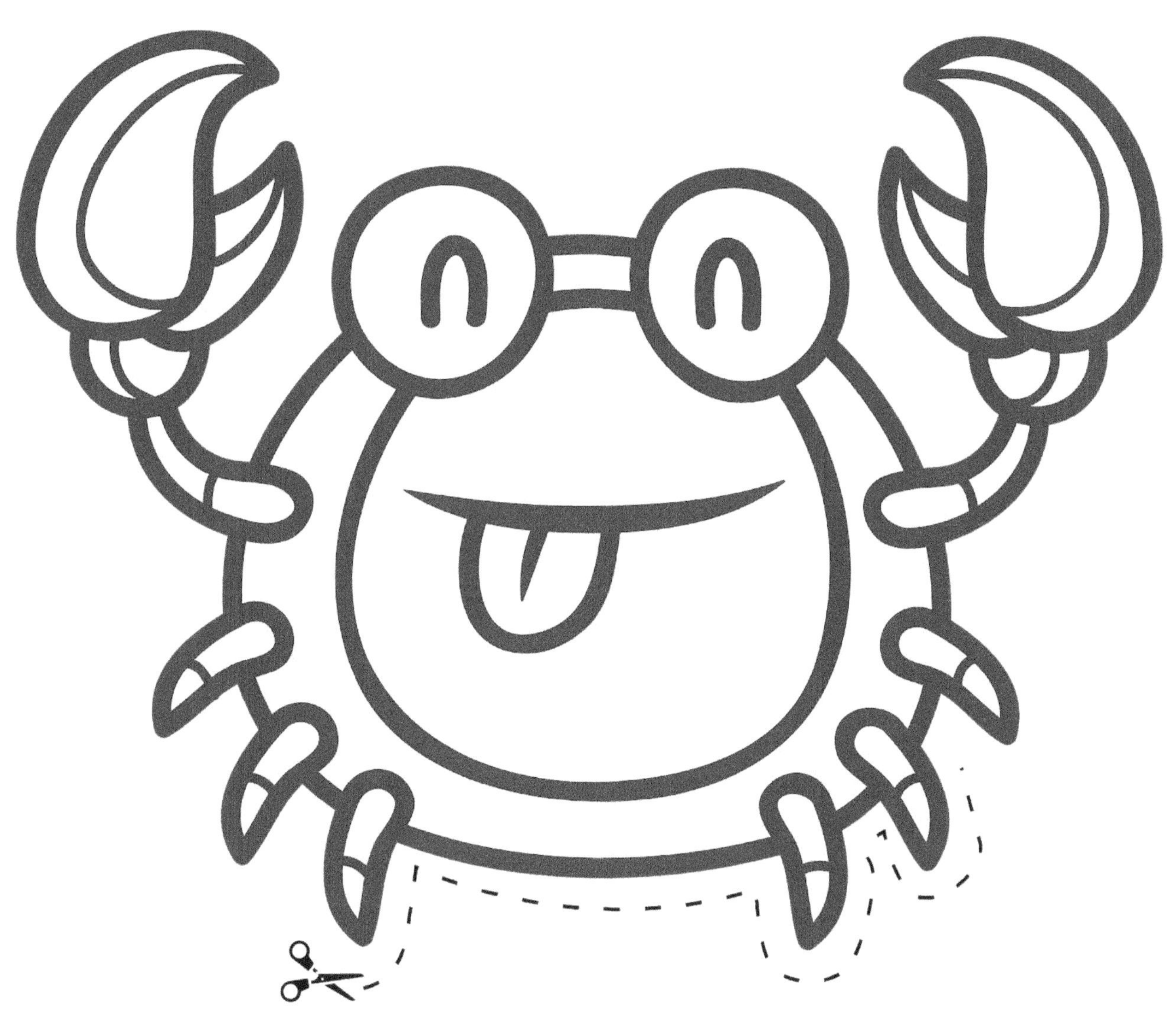

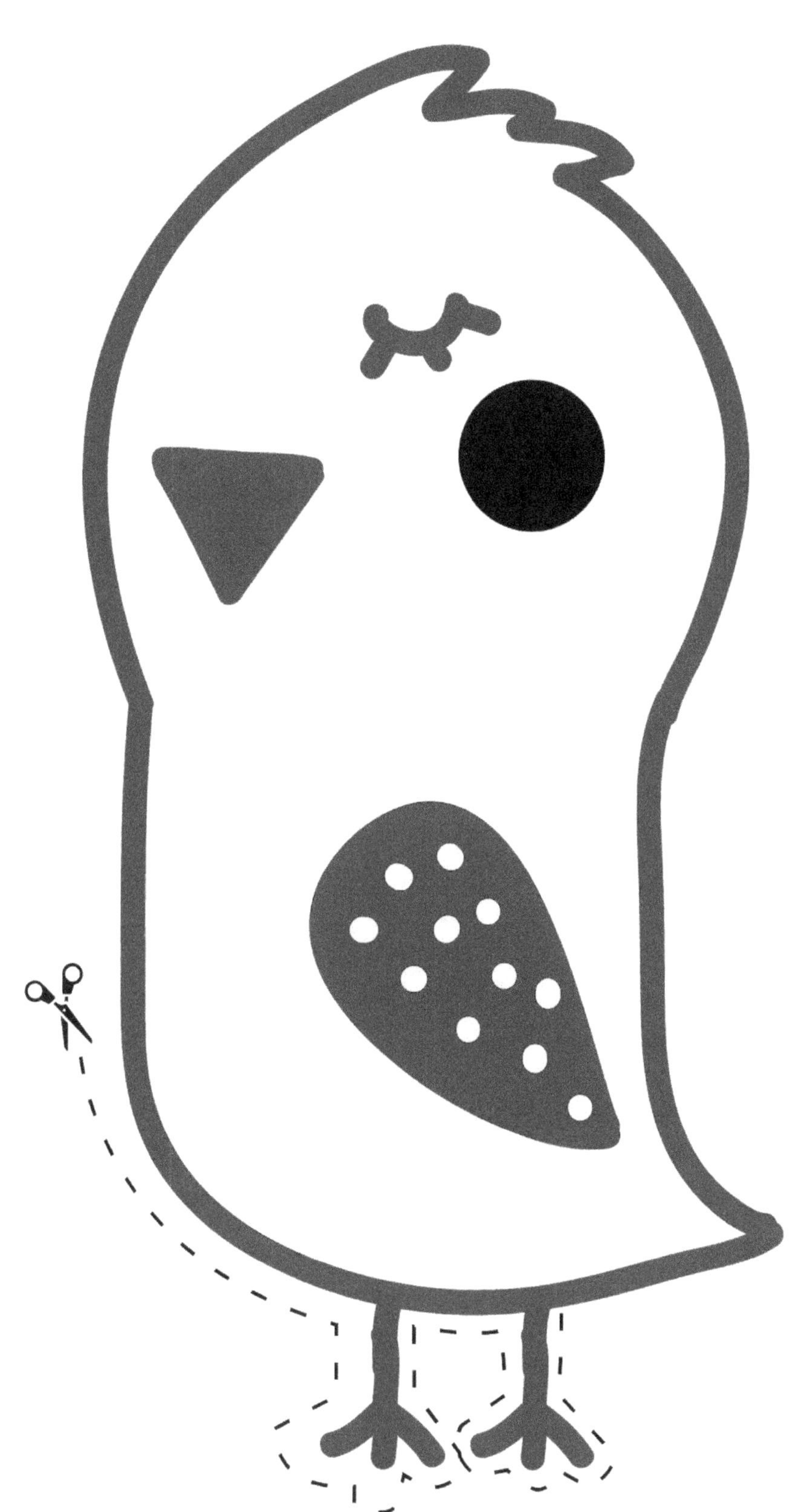

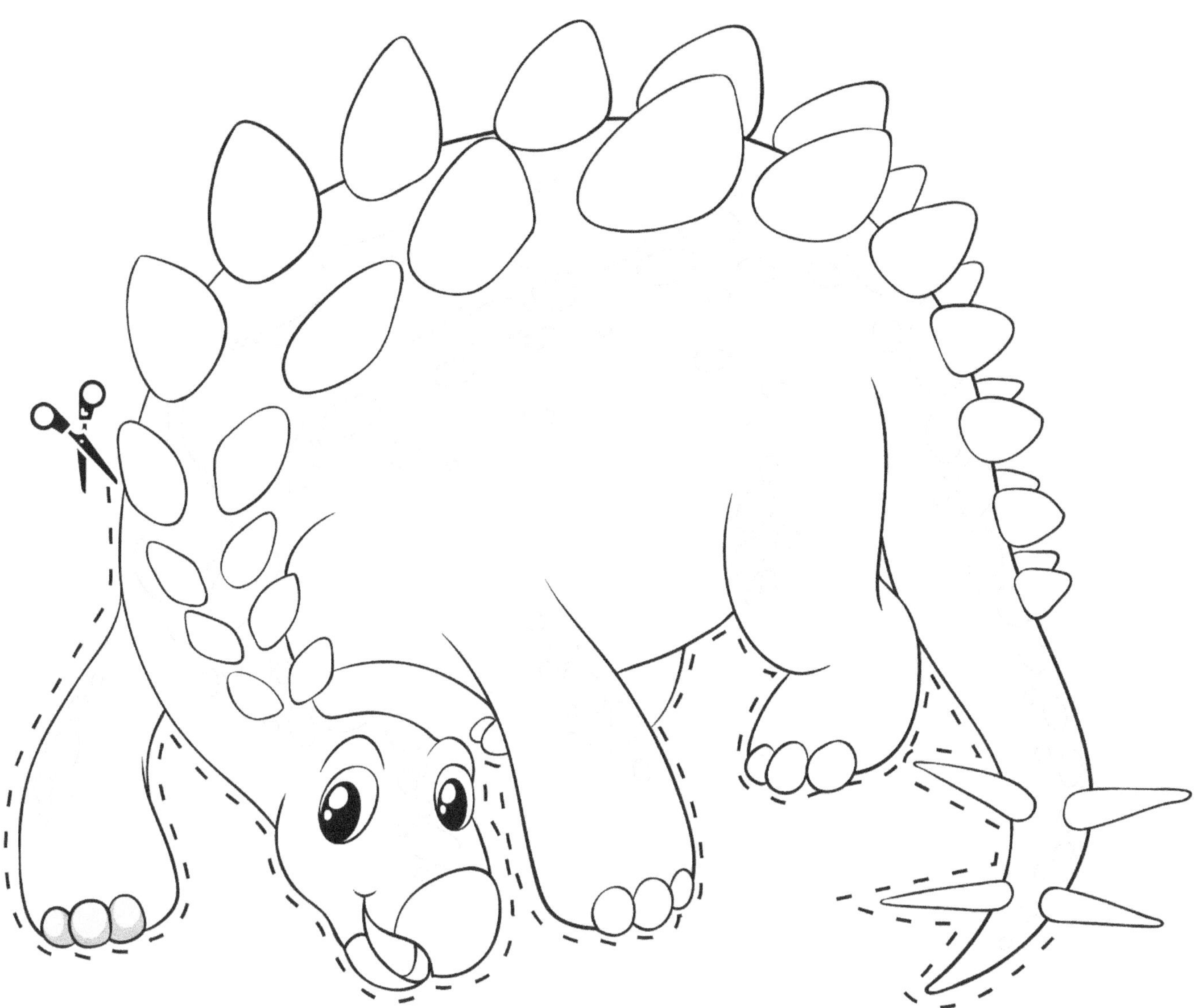

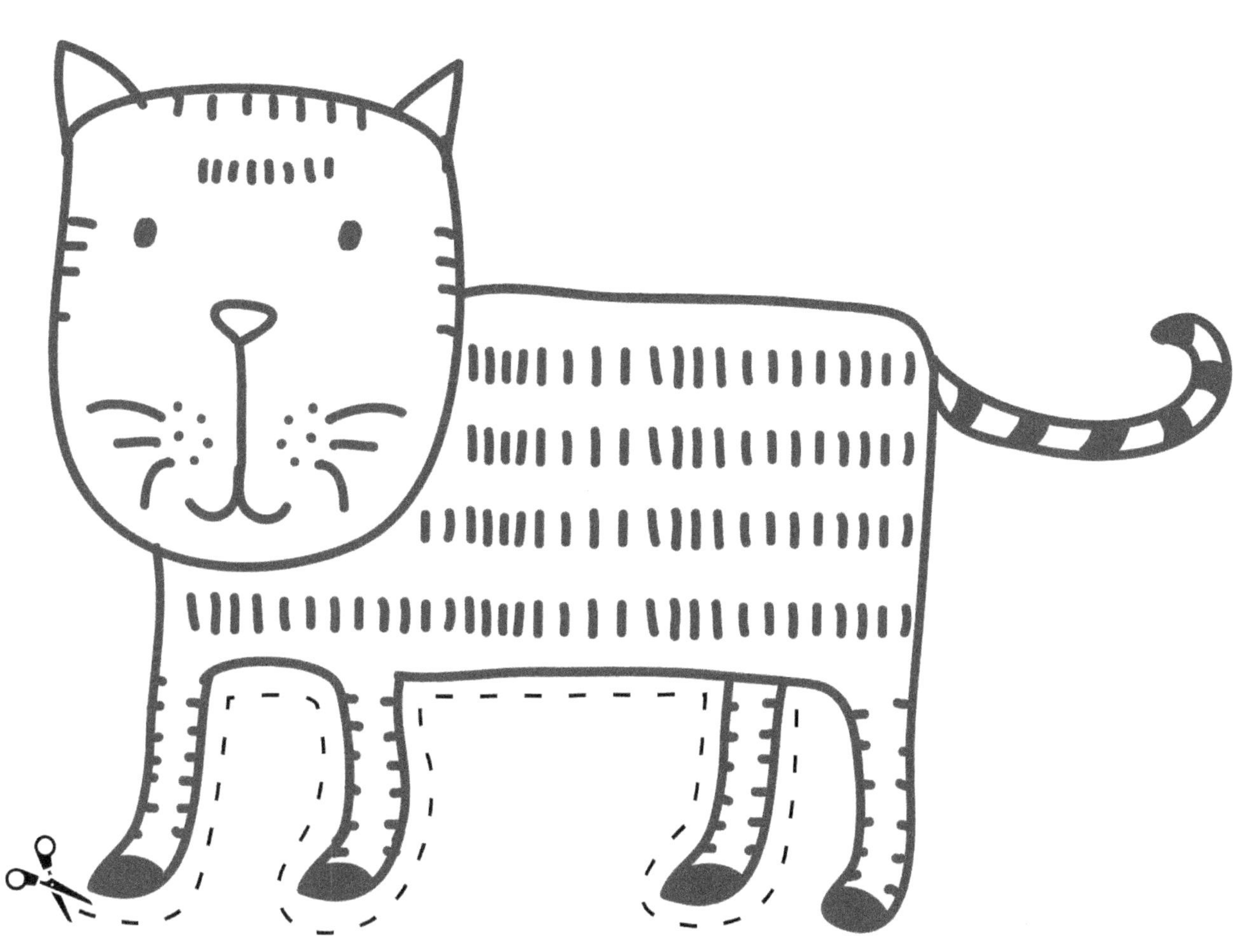

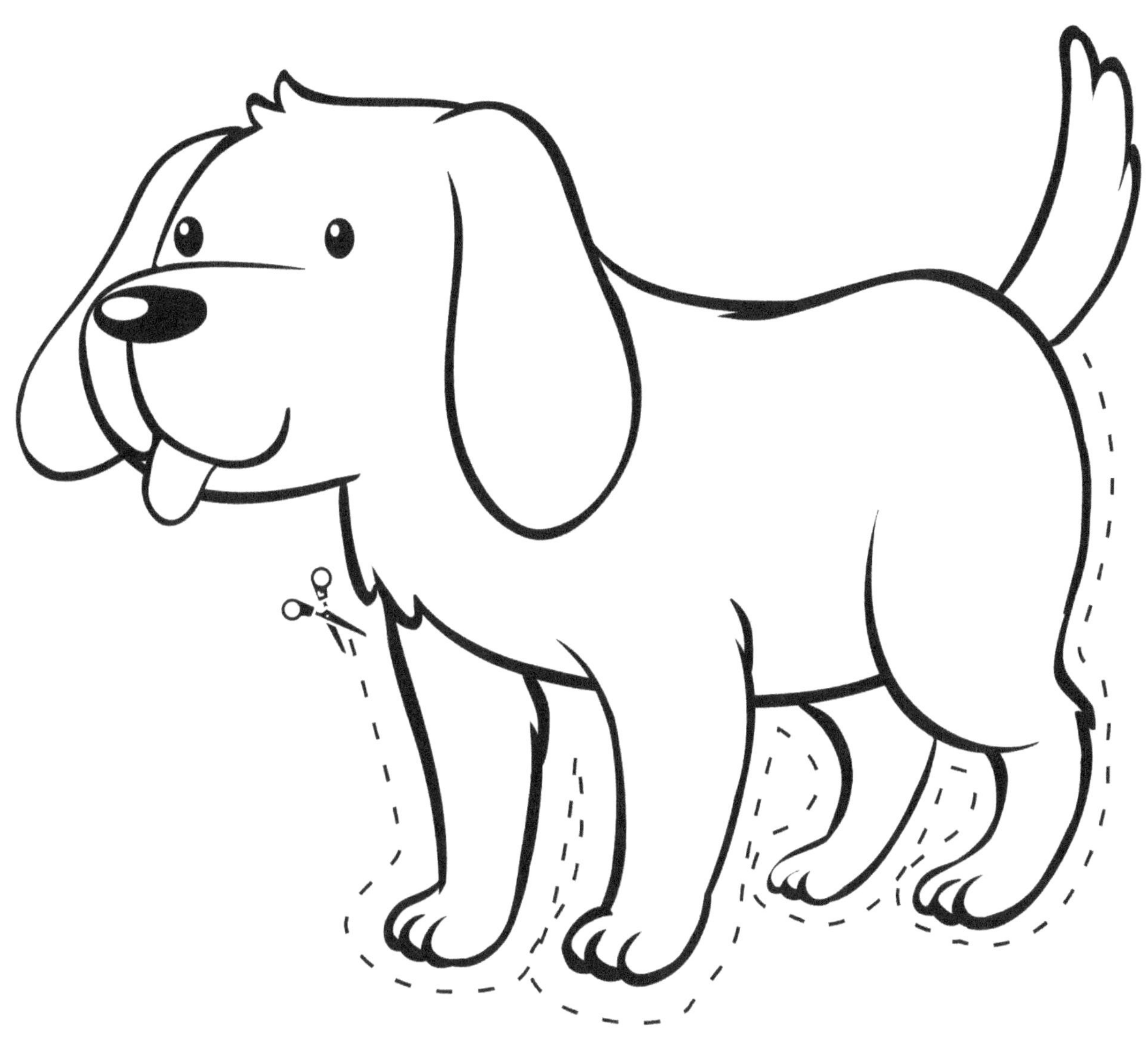

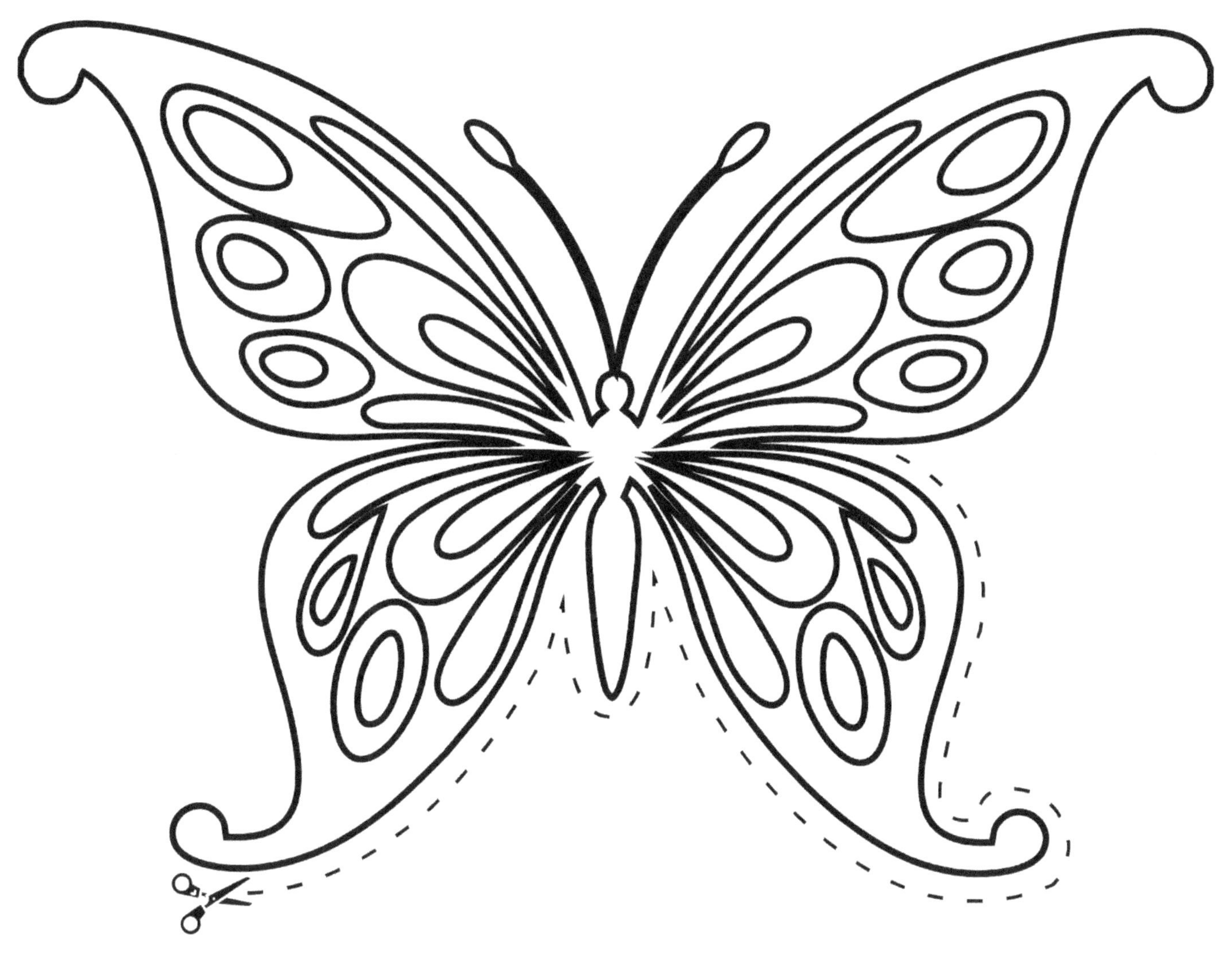

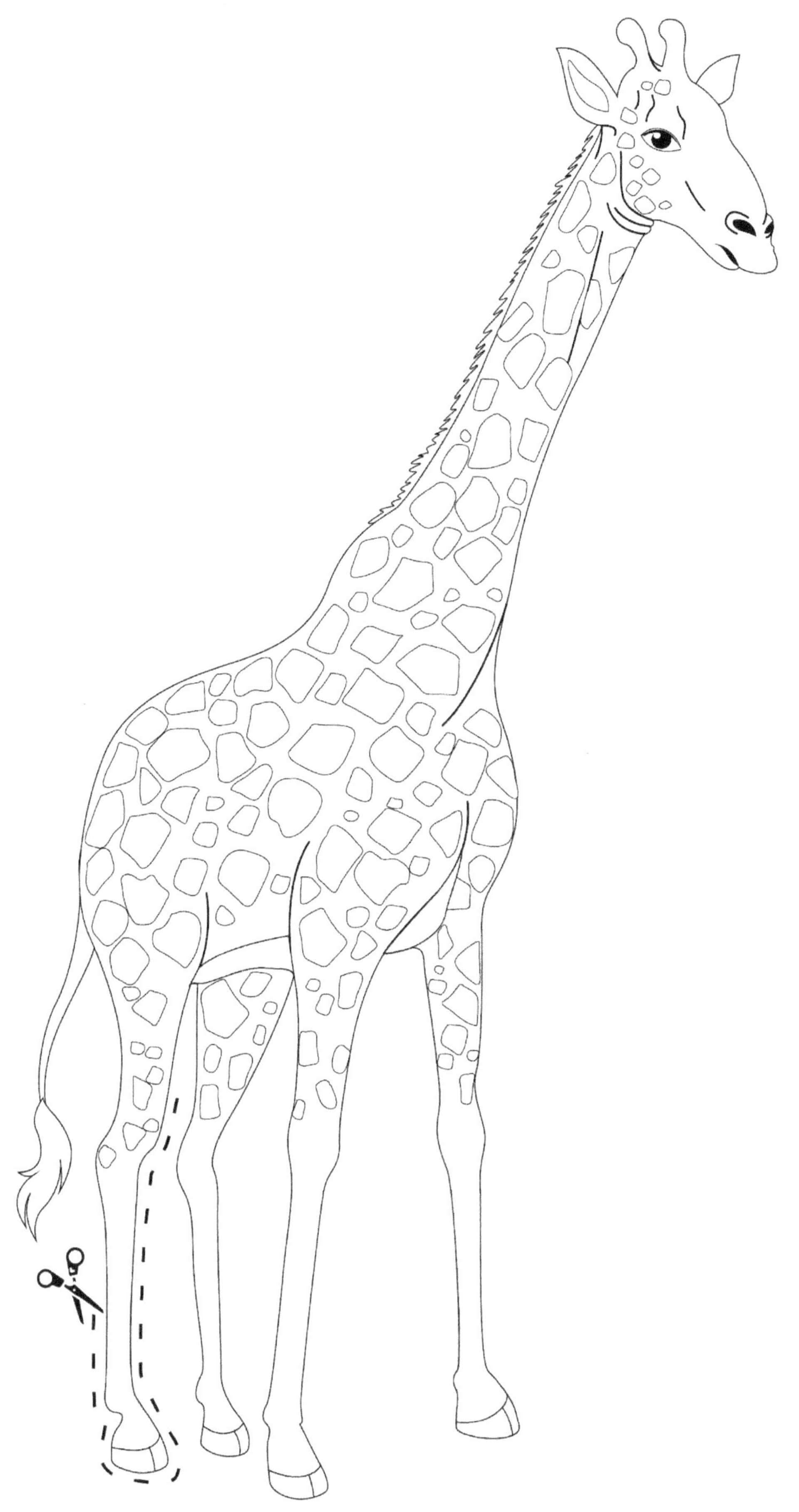

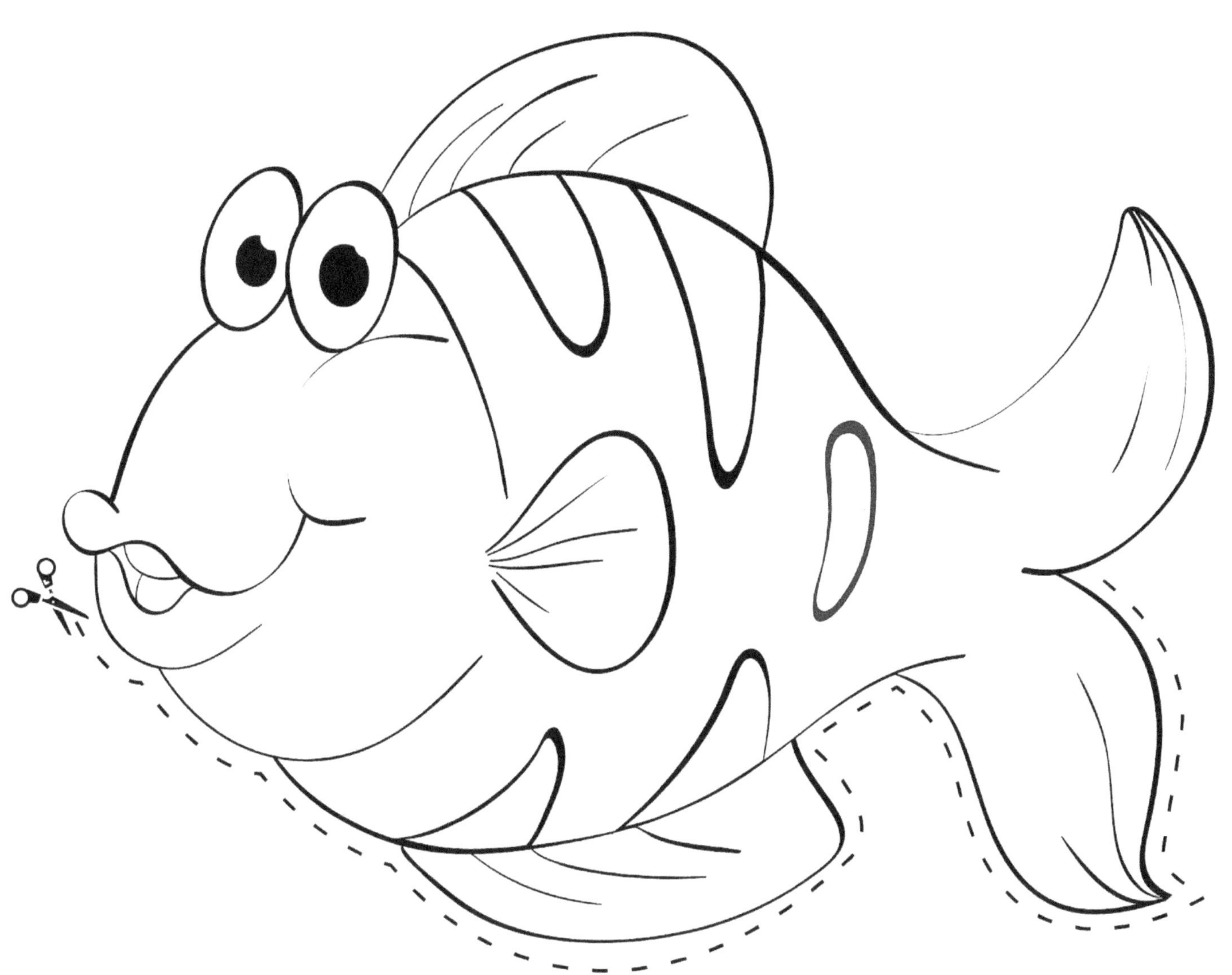

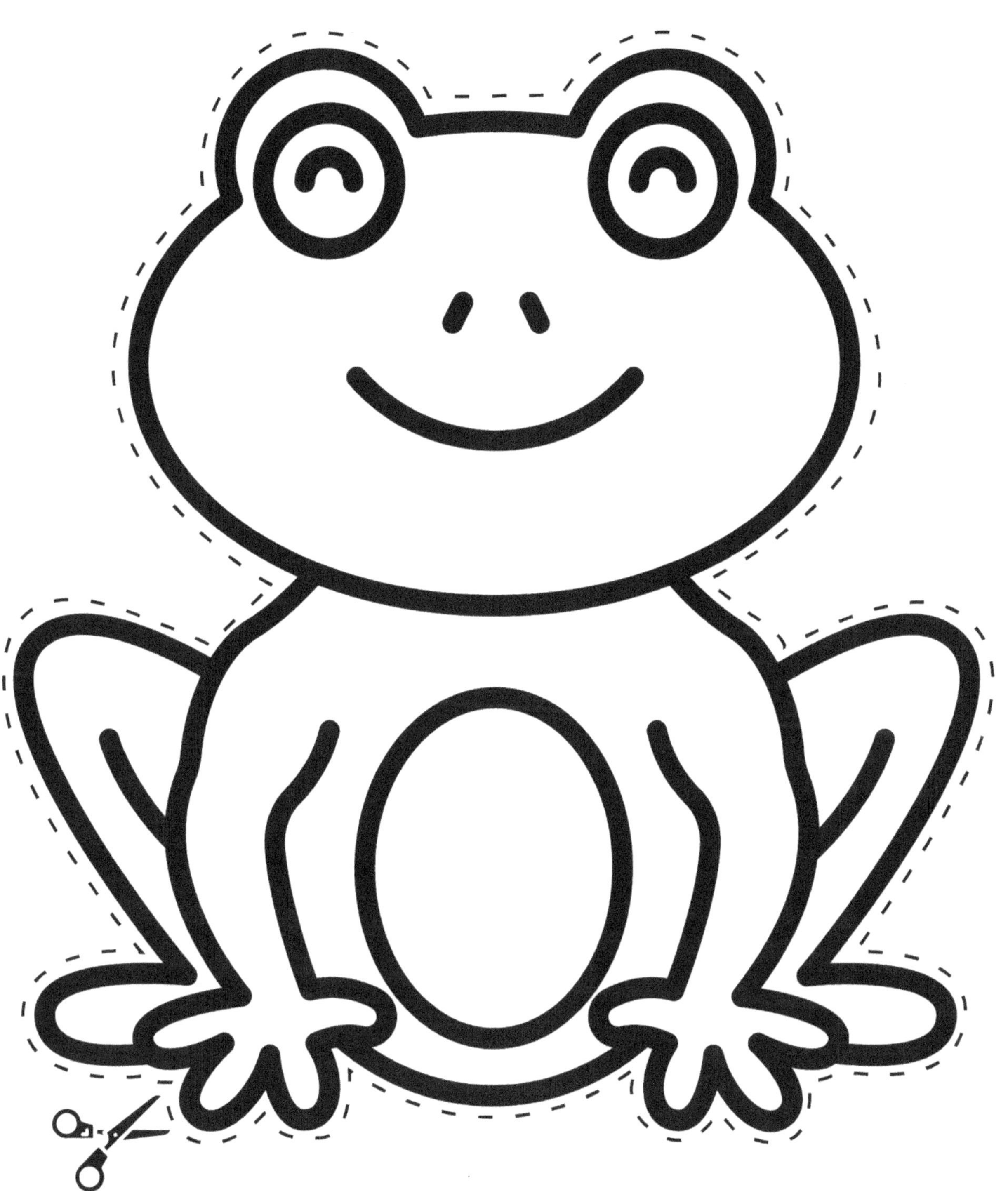

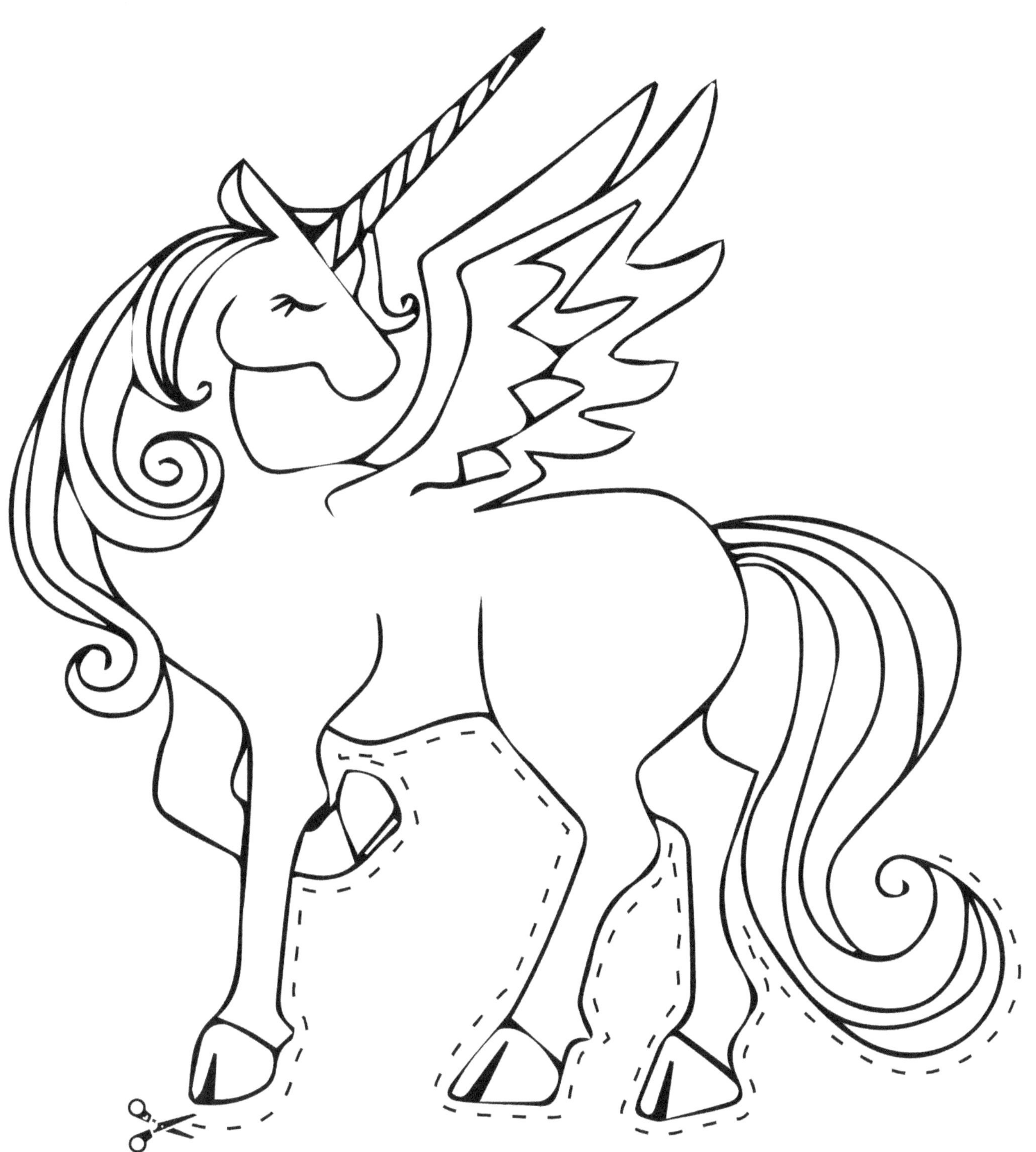

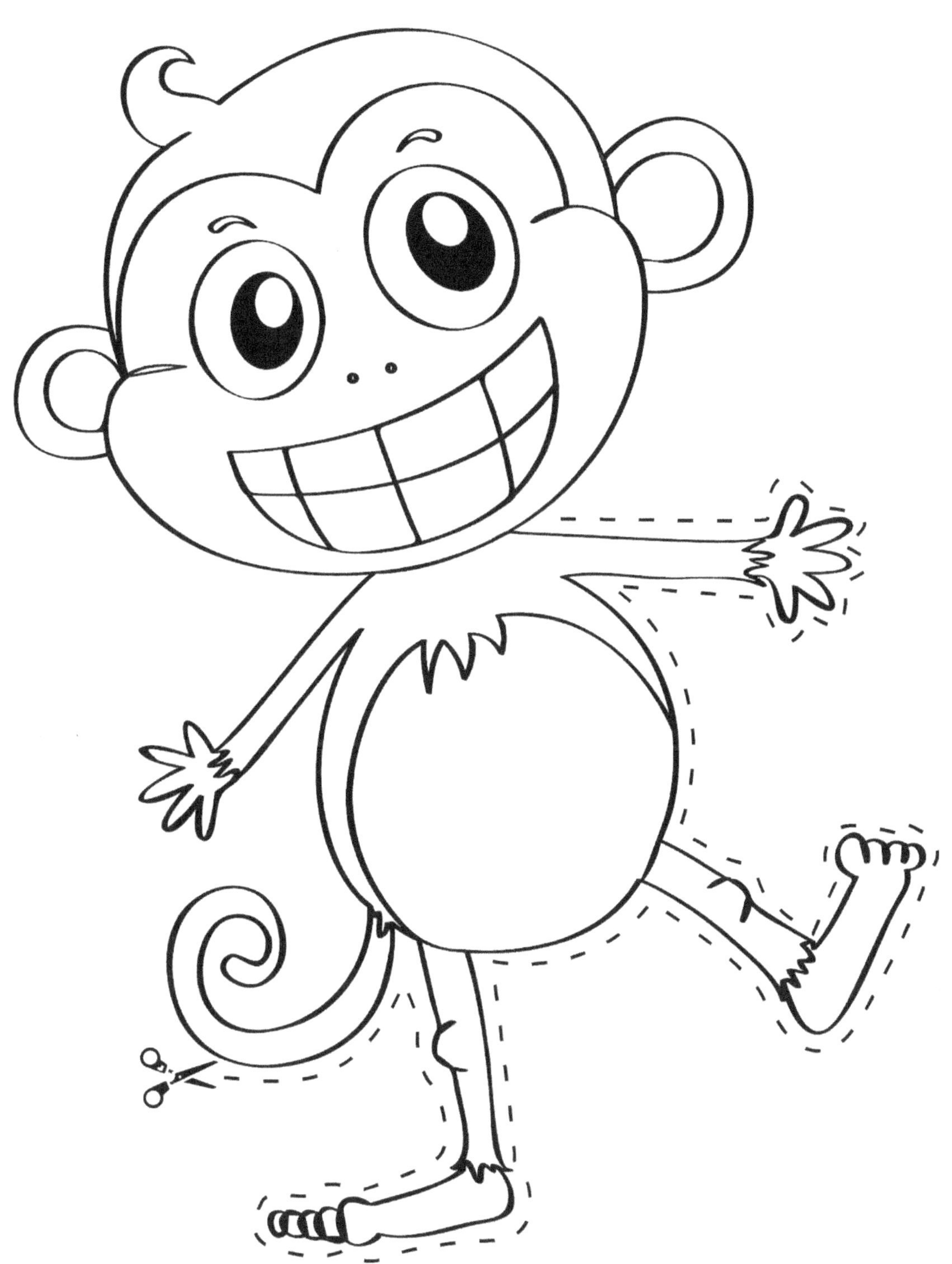